Praise for *Charting the Course*

"When I scuba dive, I always go with a Master Diver. Smart divers always go with experienced leaders. Divers never 'go it alone.' When it comes to church planting, Tim Beltz in *Charting the Course* brings the voice of a proven leader. You don't have to go it alone to start a church. Smart church planters will listen to this experienced leader and utilize his advice. Tim brings the legal and business issues of starting a church. He answers vital questions of "what do I have to do?" and "how can I keep out of legal pitfalls?" For every church planter, this is a must-read."

> **Dr. David Fletcher**, founder XPastor, author of *People Patterns and Crisis Leadership*, and a pastor for 35 years in churches from 1,000 to 8,000

"Few church planters are skilled in ensuring that their church plants are on solid legal footing. Thankfully, we have leaders like Tim Beltz, a seasoned veteran, who excel at helping church planters set up their churches legally. In *Charting the Course*, Tim Beltz carefully guides the church planter through the necessary legal steps to establishing a new church. I only wish I had this book at the beginning of my church plant! I highly recommend this work to every church planter."

> **Brian Howard**, CEO of PastorGuide, Chairman of the Board of Acts 29 Network

"Church planting, in my estimation, is one of the most difficult roles in Christian ministry. Frankly many church planters just don't make it. There are a variety of reasons for this, and much has been written to address the issue. There is one area however that little has been said or written; all the legal documents that need to be created along with other foundational documents that will aid a church planter in navigating the turbulent waters of church planting. I have known (and worked with) Tim Beltz for more than a decade and can attest to his credentials and experience as an accomplished Executive Pastor and business leader. Additionally, his many years of service as a Coast Guard officer uniquely qualify him to speak to this critical area of church planning. *Charting the Course: "How-To" Navigate the Legal Side of a Church Plant* is a must-read for all church planters."

Dave Kraft, Pastor, Author and Leadership Coach

"*Charting the Course* is a much-needed gift to church planters. This concise and practical guide is warm, inspiring, and approachable—much like its author. When we unwrap this gift from Tim Beltz, we will find the legal basics of starting a new church in a simple manner. This book will help church planters navigate the legal waters in a safe and biblical way."

Scott Thomas, Director of U.S. Church Planting, C2C Network

"What a needed book! The legal, logistical, management, and business steps in establishing a church plant are essential—and actually a way of honoring God by reflecting his attributes in how we go about them. But there are almost no resources on how to navigate them effectively. Now comes Tim Beltz's book, which is a trustworthy yet concise and highly readable guide for any church planter. Highly recommended."

Matt Perman, Author of *What's Best Next* and founder, whatsbestnext.com

"Charting the Course is a clear, rich, and necessary book. In it, Tim faithfully reminds us of where our true citizenship lies and how that informs our faithful, appropriate, and legal navigation through the kingdom of this world. This should be mandatory reading for every church planter as well as for the leaders of churches sending them out."

Jamin Stinziano, Lead Pastor, Summit Church

"Tim Beltz is a gift to the church. While so much has been written on missional theology and practice over the last few decades, there are very few resources available on how to navigate the complex legal structures that support this vision. In my experience these 'merely human' issues tend to be the primary areas that frustrate and even sink many well-intentioned church planters and pastoral teams. I'm so excited to see this resource finally get into the hands of ministry leaders who desperately need the wisdom offered in this book!"

Brandon Shields, Lead Pastor, Soma Church, Indianapolis, IN

Praise for the "How-To" Series

"The Sojourn Network 'How-To' books are a great combination of biblical theology and practical advice, driven by a commitment to the gospel and the local congregation. Written by the local church for the local church — just the job!"

> **Tim Chester**, pastor of Grace Church Boroughbridge, faculty member of Crosslands Training, and author of over 40 books

"This series brings pastoral wisdom for everyday life in the church of Jesus Christ. Think of these short, practical books as the equivalent of a healthy breakfast, a sandwich and apple for lunch, and a family enjoying dinner together. The foundational theology is nutritious, and the practical applications will keep the body strong."

> **Dr. David Powlison**, Executive Director of CCEF; senior editor, Journal of Biblical Counseling; author of *Good and Angry: Redeeming Anger* and *Making All Things New: Restoring Joy to the Sexually Broken*

"Most leaders don't need another abstract book on leadership; we need help with the 'how-to's.' And my friends in the Sojourn Network excel in this area. I've been well served by their practical ministry wisdom, and I know you will be too."

> **Bob Thune**, Founding Pastor, Coram Deo Church, Omaha, NE, author of *Gospel Eldership* and co-author of *The Gospel-Centered Life*

"I cannot express strongly enough what a valuable resource this is for church planters, church planting teams, and young churches. The topics that are addressed in these books are so needed in young churches. I have been in ministry and missions for over 30 years, and I learned a lot from reading. Very engaging and very practical!"

Larry McCrary, Co-Founder and Director of The
Upstream Collective

"There are many aspects of pastoral ministry that aren't (and simply can't) be taught in seminary. Even further, many pastors simply don't have the benefit of a brotherhood of pastors that they can lean on to help them navigate topics such as building a healthy plurality of elders or working with artists in the church. I'm thankful for the men and women who labored to produce this series, which is both theologically-driven and practically-minded. The Sojourn Network "How-To" series is a great resource for pastors and church planters alike."

Jamaal Williams, Lead Pastor of Sojourn Midtown,
Louisville, KY

"HOW-TO" NAVIGATE THE LEGAL
SIDE OF A CHURCH PLANT

Charting

THE

Course

Tim Beltz

Series Editor: Dave Harvey

Charting the Course
"How-To" Navigate the Legal Side of a Church Plant

© 2018 Tim Beltz
All rights reserved.

A publication of Sojourn Network Press in Louisville, KY. For more books by Sojourn Network, visit us at sojournnetwork.com/store.

Cover design: Josh Noom & Benjamin Vrbicek
Interior design: Benjamin Vrbicek

Trade paperback ISBN: 978-1732055230

All emphases in Scripture quotations have been added by the author.

The Sojourn Network book series is dedicated to the pastors, elders, and deacons of Sojourn Network churches. Because you are faithful, the church will be served and sent as we plant, grow, and multiply healthy churches that last.

"Making what ought to be, what is!"

— *Rear Admiral Howard Gehring,*
USCG (retired)

CONTENTS

My Story
Why Bother?
Justice
Diligence
Wisdom
Modeling Matters

Stewarding Resources
Submitting to Authority
Subverting the Temptation of Expedience

Preparation
Legal Steps
Commercial/Business Steps
Management Steps

1. Articles of Incorporation Guide

SERIES PREFACE

Why should the Sojourn Network publish a "How-To" series?

It's an excellent question, since it leads to a more personal and pertinent question for you: *Why should you bother to read any of these books?*

Sojourn Network, the ministry I am honored to lead, exists to plant, grow, and multiply healthy networks, churches, and pastors. Therefore, it seems only natural to convert some of our leader's best thinking and practices into written material focusing on the "How-To" aspects of local church ministry and multiplication.

We love church planters and church planting. But we've come to believe it's not enough to do assessments and fund church plants. We must also help, equip, and learn from one another in order to be good shepherds and leaders. We must stir up one another to the good work of leading churches towards their most fruitful future.

That's why some books will lend themselves to soul calibration for ministry longevity, while others will examine the riggings of specific ministries or specialized mission. This is essential work to building ministries *that last*. But God has also placed it on our hearts to share our mistakes and most fruitful practices so that others might improve upon what we have done. This way, everyone wins.

If our prayer is answered, this series will bring thoughtful, pastoral, charitable, gospel-saturated, church-grounded, renewal-based "practice" to the rhythms of local church life and network collaboration.

May these "How-To" guides truly serve you. May they arm you with new ideas for greater leadership effectiveness. Finally, may they inspire you to love Jesus more and serve his people with grace-inspired gladness, in a ministry that passes the test of time.

Dave Harvey
President, Sojourn Network

INTRODUCTORY LETTER

Dear Church Leader,

I am but a simple sailor. Vocationally speaking, I resemble Peter the Apostle in his earlier years. I am not yet a theologian, nor a scholar — perhaps I never will be. I see ministry through the lenses of organization, structure, and sequence with a mixture of both normative perspectives and existential moments. My former boss, Admiral Gehring, often said we are, "Making what ought to be, what is." This mantra became my operational imperative when I first heard him declare it a quarter-century ago.

What follows in this book has been observed, processed, and refined from this vantage point.

I love church planters. To begin the planting adventure, one must possess a clear calling, great courage, strong conviction, and multiple forms of perseverance. Only the right blending of righteousness and insanity can lure a man into a role where each day he learns more about what he doesn't know. These guys are lunatics. Therefore, I love celebrating and serving them.

But church planters need a certain kind of perseverance to navigate the nuances embedded in the legal and governmental regulation of establishing a new church. This is a distant shore from the doctrinal, theological, and pastoral passions that delivered them into ministry. Just the thought of having to meet with an attorney or certified public accountant, with their exorbitant fees and billable hours, can prompt a cold shudder down the church planter's spine.

Here is the irony: Your stewardship of the church plant and the faithful fulfillment of your call make you duty-bound to ensure these things are done and done with precision. This task probably feels like you are being asked to do the impossible, like sailing a dinghy through stormy, wave-breaking seas. Let me encourage you, if this seems overwhelming to you, that's entirely understandable. In fact, I wrote this "how-to" guide for the overwhelmed.

Charting the Course is meant to serve as a trustworthy companion to help church planters guide their new church plant into sound legal and business waters. My long career in and around church plants has taught me that the legal requirements don't, and never will, go away. Many a church planter could testify that ignorance is not an option. You must steer your church into safe, legal waters. While the challenge is formidable, this book will help demystify the legal language and chart the course for your church plant.

Partnered in the gospel,
Tim Beltz
Captain, US Coast Guard (retired)

PHILOSOPHY

ORGANIZATION WITH VIRTUE

God's plan for fulfilling the Great Commission will primarily utilize the life, ministry, and multiplication of local churches across the globe. God's call to individual church planters must resonate deep in their hearts and stir them to plant against the enemies of sin, flesh, and Satan. The calling resonates deeper as the Holy Spirit works in our ordinary yet vital spiritual disciplines of Scripture, prayer, meditation, working with our local church leadership, and community life. As the church planter matures into his calling and the affirmation from his local church grows, the planter begins the process of planting out from his local church. And when it comes together, a newly planted church enables a planter and the new church to serve as ambassadors for the glorious cause of gospel mission (2 Corinthians 5:11–20).

My Story

Church planting and coaching those who plant is familiar territory for me. God has afforded me the opportunity to assist scores of church planters while serving as the executive pastor (XP) at both Mars Hill Church and Sojourn Community Church. During the Mars Hill season of my life from 2007 – 2013, I spent time with Acts 29 planters in their church planting training pipeline as a coach, teacher, and trainer in different venues.

Again, when I served in the XP role at Sojourn Community Church from 2013 – 2016, I became familiar with Sojourn Network as a board member and network strategist while assisting Sojourn Network church planters. During these roles, I worked with church planters by dispensing technical and professional advice on the legal and organizational sides of church planting. And now, this has become my fulltime service to the kingdom of God as I continue to consult with church planters, pastors, and leaders from around the country. I love what I do so much that it feels scandalous to be paid for it — almost.

The past decade of studying and working directly with churches in the start-up phase has been instructive to me. I now have a better grasp on how and why the complexity of the start-up phase feels so daunting for leaders not trained in legal and business aspects of church planting. The intimidation is not imaginary, but instead very real for most church planters. If I could read their mind, I suspect they'd be thinking either, "Let's just get this over as fast and painlessly as possible," or "Whom can I find to do this work for me?" It is extremely rare to hear a church planter say, "These legal and business start-up tasks motivate me, refresh me, and seem to provide a great missional opportunity to interact with people that I otherwise would seldom encounter!"

Therefore, my hope is for church planters to re-frame their start-up activities as a vital part of their ambassadorship to their local community for expanding gospel mission, instead of a necessary evil.

Why Bother?

Let's drill down a bit more into the specifics. A church planter must pursue godliness in planting by adhering to several overarching biblical principles. These principles will guide their journey in dealing with matters involving the Secretary of State for your specific state, the Internal Revenue Service, and officials at your local bank. As we organize church ministries before the eyes of

Your excellence, virtue, integrity, and competence should confirm the reality of what we say we believe.

the world, we are called to make clear statements about the Savior we serve by how we serve.

The people we interact with are not just officials, but they are part of your church plant's mission. Your excellence, virtue, integrity, and competence should confirm the reality of what we say we believe. Does that seem like an exaggerated goal or setting the bar too high? Consider these biblical principles applied to the who, what, and how of church planting and their impact on the way you set up the church plant:

First, a church planter must be "above reproach" (1 Timothy 3:2–7). Think of this statement as having a broad and narrow meaning. Broadly, "above reproach" operates first as an overarching value that further defines and elaborates on each of the following qualities. The phrase calls for a pattern of life that confirms the gospel preached by the elder.

Narrowly, "above reproach" means no one could charge you for breaking a law of God. Therefore, we should think of the laws of the land in which we live as the "floor" or a minimum requirement for all people. But as followers of Jesus Christ, we operate at a level far above this "floor" as Jesus made clear in the Sermon on the Mount (Matthew 5–7). Jesus's bar is high and not easily scaled.

For an elder to be above reproach means he complies with the governmental, regulatory, organizational, and commercial requirements in an honest, accurate, and conscionable manner. When someone looks at the church's financial statements or bylaws, these documents should make a clear statement that the elder-planter does not see himself above or beyond the law. He is under the law and appropriately submitted to it. Where laws are just, he can submit to them with gratitude that he lives in a land where the rule of law includes provisions for churches.

Second, a church plant must bring organization for the church members and the local community to flourish. God ordained organization as a part of humankind's essential work. In the opening chapters of Genesis, God creates a beautiful universe including our world with sequence and order. He organizes his creation with sequence (night versus day, land versus sea, etc.) and he gives order to his creation placing humankind as his image bearers, the pinnacle of creation. Humans are meant to rule with God over God's creation bringing God's image physically to every part of the world for God's continuing greatness and glory. God's command in Genesis 1:28 describes this:

> And God blessed them. And God said to them, "Be fruitful and multiply and fill the earth and subdue it, and have dominion over the fish of the sea and over the birds of the heavens and over every living thing that moves on the earth."

First God created and organized, then instructed humanity to continue to create (or re-create from God's creation) and organize with subduing and extending dominion, otherwise known as work. God made a perfect and sinless creation, yet it was an unfinished creation. This is humankind's task, to finish God's creation through fruitful living and work with God as a vice-regent.[1]

Genesis 1:28 is called the 'Cultural or Creation Mandate' because it gives the grand purpose of life to humankind. We are to know God and live (and work) for his glory. But sin enters the Garden of Eden (Genesis 3) through Adam and Eve, and humankind's purpose becomes tainted by sin. Work is now about survival and self-glory rather than joy, purpose, and cooperation with God. The later Great Commission not only rescues us from our sins, but also restores us to a

---

[1] For more, see T. Desmond Alexander, *From Eden to the New Jerusalem*, (Grand Rapids: Kregel, 2010).

meaningful life with God. Our life with God should be filled with work, including organizing and bringing order in the world for God's glory and the subsequent flourishing of humankind.

Your apprehensions about the business and legal sides of establishing your church plant are not just gaps in confidence, but evidence of a fallen world. These challenges are an opportunity to thrive through trusting God amongst fallen people, systems, and laws to continue to organize well for the kingdom of God. Our God consistently brings his people to the work of organizing throughout the Scriptures including: Adam's naming the of the animals (Genesis 2:20), Noah's building and filling the Ark (Genesis 6:9–22), Joseph's stewardship of resources before famine (Genesis 47:13–27), Moses organizing Israelites for leadership and justice matters (Exodus 18), the construction of the temple (1 Kings 6; 1 Chronicles 29), and so on. In the New Testament, the early church faced the need for better organization to feed the Greek widows with efficiency and fairness, which also prompted the establishment of deacons (Acts 6).

> **When the planting of a church follows the governmentally prescribed paths to maintain order and organization within a country, we bless our neighbors.**

Organizing the local church in a planned, legal, and deliberate manner follows God's creating and his cultural mandate to us. When the planting of a church follows the governmentally prescribed paths to maintain order and organization within a country, we bless our neighbors. The required steps and sequence result in the legal establishment of a new church registered and ready to operate in the broader marketplace of our culture and society.

The act of getting organized requires both physical and mental tasks. Physical tasks for the formation of a church plant include completing forms and submitting them to the correct authorities. The mental tasks precede the physical ones as they deal with envisioning a particular structure and way of organizing the church. There are multiple questions and matters to decide before your paperwork can be completed and submitted to your state. Notice the order and sequence — even the government follows God ordained patterns.

Third, the church plant must model the "message of the gospel" through every stage of the legal and business planting process. The tenets of our faith must transcend every facet of the church organization and operation. Simply said, our practices should exemplify justice, diligence, and wisdom in every transaction and relationship as these gospel imperatives reflect the goodness of Christ's redeemed and being redeemed church.

Justice

The Lord delights in justice (Proverbs 21:3). The church can be an agent of this redemptive justice. Business and ministry must be conducted with fairness, honesty, and a sense of awareness and action for the less fortunate. There are many ways to inhabit this sense of justice from the very beginning of planting.

The church can start with compensating staff and vocational pastors fairly and appropriately for their labors. Treat vendors and Sunday venues respectfully and honestly. Furthermore, a church can consider their responsibilities for justice and mercy inside the church among its membership; and then address the issues to the surrounding community as well. Things like keeping the facility maintained with a gospel-mission mindset, helping neighboring churches with legal matters from your expertise, and even landscaping in a way to cultivate safety and community can bolster the more direct justice and mercy efforts conducted by church members on a personal level.

Self-awareness to the needs and concerns of the city, in addition to keen insight to geographical "place" of the church, will enable your church plant to serve and reach with justice over "tone-deafness" to your surroundings. This is the corporate part of learning how to apply Micah 6:8:

> He has told you, O man, what is good;
>   and what does the LORD require of you
> but to do justice, and to love kindness,
>   and to walk humbly with your God?

Neighbors, businesses, government officials, other churches, are all watching, and justice speaks a beautiful word about our God.

Diligence

The Lord expects us to productively use whatever knowledge and resources given to us, no matter how great or small (Luke

25:14–15). The antonyms for diligence are: disregard, carelessness, neglect, indifference, and thoughtlessness. Application of this principle means there are no alibis or excuses because, "We didn't know," or "We are just a church in the start-up phase." Pleading ignorance or incompetence doesn't invite an extension of grace from a government official or marketplace vendor — only scorn and reproach.

Through your diligence in resources and knowledge, you can not only win favor from external officials but also inspire confidence in the leadership of your church internally. This is vital, as you are asking people to invest their future time, talent, and treasure into the growing church plant. People can see when things are done with excellence in the details and the simplicity of Proverbs 21:5a, "The plans of the diligent lead surely to abundance," speaks volumes.

Wisdom

To exercise justice and diligence as a gospel witness, we need wisdom as our final imperative. Throughout the Scriptures, wisdom is presented as the gift of God through life-long experience in righteous fear of God (Proverbs 1:7). Wisdom does not just come from expertise. Wisdom is a gift from God (James 1:5).

Wisdom is necessary to navigate the planting process and win the respect of those watching your planting progress along with your core team's respect too. Reading this book among other resources and training is precisely how a wise planter seeks to glean wisdom from the experiences of others and to avoid their pitfalls. Wisdom is needed as an imperative because planting will require more than diligence or good-natured attempts at justice and righteousness. For diligence alone can still be worldly as the

Diligence and justice, with wisdom, yield a fruitful harvest.

Shrewd Manager of Luke 16:1–13 demonstrates. However, diligence and justice, with wisdom, yield a fruitful harvest. Wisdom must be gained through experience, sought from those who have gone before us, and found in arising situations through prayer and reflection.

Modeling Matters

Stories abound of the naïve (in the world of regulatory procedures), but wise church planter interacting with the civil service clerk or bank official in a fruitful manner. Once, an overzealous Fire Marshall attempted to shut down the opening Sunday of a potential church plant because of his "letter-of-the-law" interpretation of the local fire and building codes. The church plant's new building would not be able to hold a service of reasonable size because the Fire Marshall refused to issue a "conditional use" permit. The hard launch was just forty-eight hours away, and yet he refused to sign off on the building's use. Sure, the church planter was deeply concerned, but he was also composed.

In a spirit of justice, diligence, and wisdom he simply asked in person without arguing, "What do we need to do?" He respectfully asked for more detailed specifics of the Fire Marshall. When the church planter detailed out each problem with action steps in order to observe the law, he rallied his church plant to the list of infractions. A flood of volunteers responded, swept in, and completed the Fire Marshall's checklist within a day. The impressed Fire Marshall immediately issued the permit. And to everyone's surprise, he showed up at the first worship service. Justice, diligence, and wisdom of the gospel had won the day and modeled the way for the future of this young church plant.

The unusual and odd journey into the halls of government and commerce for the start-up of a church can become an early opportunity to be "the light of the world" in the local community (Matthew 5:14). In a world where so many people and businesses "game" the system to circumvent the law and the disadvantage of others, the virtues of this church plant provoked the curiosity of this Fire Marshall. This is what happens when the world tastes a little "salt" and sees a little "light" in the way the church operates with gospel imperatives.

PRINCIPLES

STEWARDING, SUBMITTING, AND SUBVERTING

Like a three-strand cord that is not easily broken (Ecclesiastes 4:12), there are three biblical principles for a church planter to establish the church legally:

1. Steward the resources of the church plant.
2. Submit to governing authorities.
3. Subvert the temptation of expedience.

Stewarding Resources

A church is entrusted with various resources (financial, facilities, staff and volunteers, etc.), all of which need to be managed with care and skill (i.e., worked or stewarded before God, Genesis 1:28). And stewardship starts with legally establishing your church as a nonprofit and tax-exempt corporation. This unleashes a number of positive resource conserving outcomes. As a church qualifies as a public charity under Internal Revenue Code 501(c)(3), these outcomes include:

- Eligible for federal exemption from payment of corporate income tax (except on income derived from unrelated business income like renting church facilities for business purposes).
- In most instances, do not pay state corporate income, franchise, excise, use, and sales tax.
- Individual and corporate donors offered a tax deduction for their charitable donations.
- Real property (land and buildings) exempted from state property taxes.
- Ministers, (the IRS language for pastors on the payroll) qualify for the ministerial housing allowance and may "opt out" of Social Security.
- Eligible for lower postal rates on third class bulk mailings through the US Postal Service.

Each of these outcomes will save colossal resource allocations over the lifetime of a growing church. Therefore, obtaining and establishing nonprofit and tax-exempt status correctly and quickly is important for stewardship of funds given to the Lord through your church.

Submitting to Authority

The apostle Peter speaks to the principle of our submission to the authority of the human institutions in place in 1 Peter 2:13–17. Why should we submit to secular authority? Verse 15 says, "For this is the will of God, that by doing good you should put to silence the ignorance of foolish people." If we wish to start a church, we must understand the rules and laws of the place we start said church. We are people under authority from the Lord who commands us to submit, not merely tolerate, the authorities over us (Romans 13:1). We can disagree, we can disapprove, we can protest, and when the government is grossly unrighteous, we can even disobey.

However, we must submit and honor the government in the ordinary and regulatory practices of our place (1 Peter 2:17) as we lead and organize under God's commands. The practice of submission to authority is displayed when you register with the state. Both the federal and state governments require registration for several reasons; mostly aimed to identify the "responsible officials" (owner) in the event of legal action, ensure a minimal level of organizational structure (bylaws), and collect taxes unless exempted. Churches registered as nonprofit corporations within their state and qualified under the Internal Revenue Code 501(c)(3) are exempt from a variety of taxes.

That last line was pretty significant. You need to read it again.

Furthermore, you must legally establish your church as a nonprofit corporation so your church plant can handle relationships like commercial transactions (receiving and depositing donations, obtaining a church credit card, paying staff, and vendors), hiring designers for a logo, website, other technology, and rental agreements, etc.

Subverting the Temptation of Expedience

Church planters wake up to dozens of competing priorities. Meeting space, outreach, pastoral care, core team development, sermon prep — it can easily feel like everything is urgent. With this comes the unrelenting temptation for shortcuts and corner cutting, sometimes resulting in imprudent acts of expedience.

It's difficult to forget the church planter who called me for help a few years back. He humbly confessed that he was so focused on clearing the legal hoops "quickly" that he used the Articles of Incorporation and bylaws from another church. In his rush to strike it from his to-do list, he didn't even change the name and location of the church in his application form. His expedience cost him credibility when he had to reapply for incorporation and attempt to explain his predicament to the unsympathetic clerk.

Approximately 1,000 churches are sued every month.

One lazy and careless "shortcut" created a dozen hours of new work.

Keep in mind that some statistics indicate approximately 1,000 churches are sued every month. Yes, you read that correctly, every single month in the United States. The Pew Forum on Religion and Public Life even categorizes the four different types of court cases most prevalent against churches: property disputes, employment of clergy, treatment or discipline of members, and misconduct by church staff.[1]

---

[1] "Churches in Court," *Pew Research Center*, March 31, 2011, http://www.pewforum.org/2011/03/31/churches-in-court1/.

Getting the founding documents right at start-up, can prevent many of the situations and keep the church out of court or become invaluable in legal situations. This begins with resisting unwise instincts towards expedience and replacing these feelings of rush with dedicated and patient attention to the essential details.

In my world of consulting with church planters, it brings me great joy when I see a bright and motivated church planter asking for help in the legal and business aspects of starting the church. This humility demonstrated in acknowledging one's potential ignorance and asking for help which subverts the temptation towards unwise expedience. More importantly, it prioritizes the right things at the right time and helps establish a culture of prudent decision-making.

PROCESS

YOUR FIRST STEPS

With the hope that my philosophical considerations and principles have sufficiently whetted your appetite for the main course, let's turn our attention to the question, "What exactly is the process to establish my church plant?" In broad strokes, the start of the church legally will have three major steps.

First, understand that a church planter is creating a legal entity called a nonprofit corporation. This is accomplished by filing Articles of Incorporation with the state. A nonprofit corporation is a legal entity separate and distinct from its founders and members. Thus, the church is formed into a legal entity that will manage its assets, activities, policies, and procedures. As a nonprofit corporation, the church can then enjoy limited legal liability. This means that the personal assets of the founders, directors, officers, trustees, and others in leadership positions would be protected if, for example, a lawsuit is brought against the church. An example of Articles of Incorporation is provided in Appendix One.

Second, some specific "one-time start-up tasks" are necessary for a church to move from the "registration" as a nonprofit corporation to become ready to function as a church and business entity. This involves both legal and commercial elements — all of which will be discussed below.

Lastly, a certain mentality needs to be adopted. Specifically, you must begin thinking of your launch in three distinct stages: pre-launch, launch, and post-launch. The pre-launch stage is the primary focus of this book. Pre-launch represents the time and tasks invested in completing these initial start-up tasks.

Now, let's spell it out by looking at the specific steps a church planter must take. It may help to know that many of the steps we will discuss are sequential, meaning, the completion of one step must occur before proceeding to the next one. A few of the steps are concurrent, by which I mean, they may be completed at any time. These are labeled for your convenience.

The sequence of these three major steps is broken down into the detailed steps below under four broad categories of the actions and considerations needed: Preparation, Legal, Commercial/Business, and Management.

Preparation

Before one begins the process to register a church as a nonprofit corporation, several fundamental decisions must be reached in order to complete the basic forms.

Location: Decide the location (city and state) where the church will be established. You do not need to have an actual physical meeting place (or address) for worship services; that comes later.

Name: Decide upon the corporate and legal name of your church. Check with your state's Secretary of State website to see if your naming choice is available. Corporate names must be unique — no sharing of the same church name within your state. The full and legal name of your church will appear on all your legal documents (Articles of Incorporation, Bylaws, Federal Employer Identification Number, etc.) Local, state, and governmental entities need to ensure your church has a distinct name.

For instance, there are likely hundreds or even thousands of "First Baptist Churches" across the United States. That is why your state's Secretary of State website will prompt you to discover how to customize a name. For instance, "First Baptist Church of Talladega." Check it out, fbctalladega.com — it exists.

Agent: Determine who will serve as the "registered agent" and their mailing address. The registered agent address must be located at a street address where service of process (that means where a subpoena or other legal documents could be delivered) may be personally served to the agent during normal business hours. Although the registered office is not required to be the entity's principal place of business, the registered office may not be solely a mailbox service or telephone answering service.

Governance: A basic idea of how the church will be "governed." The state wants to know if the affairs of your church will be governed by a Board of Directors or by other corporate members. There are multiple church governance models. Six of the most common are:

1. Congregation Model — members (congregation) vote and decide most major decisions.
2. Presbyterian Model — governance by elders/overseers in graded courts (local & denominational).
3. Elder Board Model — usually elected by the church members.
4. Senior Pastor Model — single leader assumes the governance functions.
5. Professional Clergy Model — often referred to as "staff-led" model.
6. Plurality of Elders Model — a "full council of elders" who may govern by electing/appointing a smaller-sized panel or board with some delegated authority.

Corporate Members: The church planter is faced with an important organization structure question right at the start. Your state likely will have a question on the Articles of Incorporation form asking if you intend to have corporate members. There are two responses: choose to have corporate members or not.

In choosing corporate members, that means these members will serve as the governing team of your church. Most church planters opt to have "no members," and then outline in the bylaws with a description of how the church will be governed depending on the model selected in "Governance" above. Many churches opt to have no members and then identify some governing body like a Board of Elders, a Leadership Council, or a Full Council of Elders.

If you choose to have corporate members that serve as your board of directors, most states require that you identify at least three directors. You will need to supply the name and contact information for each. A director must be a person (not a corporate entity), and there is no residency requirement for directors.

Most church plants will only have a single pastor . . . you, the church planter. You aren't even close to naming a governing board, however. The state Articles (or Certificate) of Incorporation requires the naming of a Board of Directors, even if this is a temporary or placeholder Board.

Without a Board, there is no incorporation or legal status under the law. Often the establishment of a temporary advisory board for one to three years is a wise workaround for this problem. Your bylaws can be fashioned in such a way as to start the nonprofit corporation with a preliminary board (required information in the Articles of Incorporation). Then the planter phases in an advisory board so that you have time to

> **Without a Board, there is no incorporation or legal status under the law.**

select, train, and commission several elders. Finally, schedule an end of the advisory board at some specified time in the future in favor of installing qualified local elders from the congregation to govern as a plurality. Similar governance strategies could be devised for non-elder led church plants.

One of the better practices I've observed for advisory boards has been to include two to four respected pastors from your sending church, denomination, or church-planting network. Invite leaders who are seasoned with organizational and administrative experience. Consider ways you can wholly submit yourself to this advisory board despite their "advisory" label. Invite them to hold you accountable in specific areas of life and ministry while regularly meeting even virtually for prayer, guidance, and support.

Fiscal Year: How do you plan to define your fiscal year? Most start-up churches use a January to December calendar year as their fiscal year. Other customary choices are July to June. If you're wondering, the selection of the fiscal year could potentially impact the timing of the annual budget process and staff performance reviews. For instance, the rationale for those opting for a July to June fiscal year could be the timing of Easter programming, budget preps, Easter travel, hiring cycles during less busy months, and summer vacations. You can easily change the fiscal year after incorporation, so there is no need to be overly anxious about the upfront selection.

Legal Steps

Legal steps require transactions with the state and the federal government. These are listed in order of sequence.

File Articles of Incorporation with your state's Secretary of State. In many states, this can be accomplished online by filing fees ranging from $100 to $250, depending on the state. Appendix 1 contains a "job aid" to guide you in the completion of the various information pieces needed for this founding document. Also included is a completed sample form. Remember, the forms are different from state-to-state.

Also, keep in mind that some states call the Articles of Incorporation a "Certificate of Incorporation."

Obtain a Federal Employer Identification Number (EIN) from the Internal Revenue Service (IRS). An EIN is simply an identification number for tax, banking, and credit purposes. It is free of charge and the required SS-4 Form can be completed online.[1] If you need additional help, Appendix 2 provides assistance in how to fill in the blanks of the SS-4 Form.

It's important to note when filling out the SS-4 that attention to detail is paramount. For instance, for line 9a, "Type of Entity," be certain to check the box labeled "Church or church-controlled organization." Otherwise, the IRS will require you to complete an annual 990 tax return because you have raised the question about whether you may be an entity other than a church.

Prepare Bylaws. Bylaws protect your church plant from control by the state and potential lawsuits from within and outside the church. Normally this step occurs a month or more after the filing of the Articles of Incorporation. The bylaws may be the most underrated founding document by a church planter. They are filled with legalese and organizational verbiage that can, at first, seem like a foreign language.

Despite the growing availability of generic templates for church bylaws, each state sets their own requirements for this important document. A church planter can save money by using a good bylaws template that is then customized to the

---

1 https://www.irs.gov/businesses/small-businesses-self-employed/apply-for-an-employer-identification-number-ein-online.

needs of this new church. However, wisdom dictates sending a draft set of bylaws to a competent attorney knowledgeable in nonprofit law, particularly as it relates to the church.

Appendix 3 speaks to the critical "must have's" in bylaws. Appendix 4 offers sample excerpts from the bylaws of various churches.

Hold a Church Organizational Board Meeting. Once your state approves your Articles of Incorporation, the church governing authorities must hold the "organizational board meeting." This meeting is essential for the newly formed church to take the first and immediate legal steps. These steps include:

1. Official appointment of the board of directors (or whatever term you use to define the governing body of your church;
2. Resolution to open a banking account (checking and savings);
3. Ratify and approve all completed corporate documents;
4. Commission/ordain the lead pastor so that he is properly licensed.

Most churches need additional time to finish bylaws and to create a few basic policies. As bylaws and policies are completed, make sure to ratify and approve all policies at your next board meeting. Also, make certain you take official meeting minutes and have them approved at the next board meeting.

Enjoy tax-exempt status as a 501(c)(3) charitable organization under the Internal Revenue Service (IRS) tax code. If the newly formed church properly prepares (and complies with) the Articles of Incorporation and Bylaws, the church automatically qualifies without completing the arduous Form 1023 or seeking a blanket exemption from a denomination or state convention. According to IRS Publication 557, churches and church ministries are "exempt automatically." This also means any contributions made to a church are "automatically qualified" as a tax write-off to the contributor, as specified in IRS Publication 526. That is exceptional news! Your church is automatically a charitable organization under IRS regulations.

There are some churches that may desire to be registered with the IRS and receive a "501(c)(3) tax-exempt recognition letter." This may become necessary under circumstances where a private foundation or corporate donor requires the letter as part of their internal procedures. Or a member or attendee making contributions to your church is suddenly audited. There are, in fact, instances in IRS audits where these contributions may not be considered as a tax write-off without the 501(c)(3) tax-exempt recognition letter. In such a case, your donor will be unable to write-off their contributions to your church.

The only protection against these events may be to complete the Form 1023 or, if applicable, seek a blanket exemption from a denomination or state convention. Keep in mind that the completion process for the Form 1023 is herculean — the IRS estimates that the prep time can exceed 120 hours. In light of this labor, you may want to confirm that you really require the tax-exemption letter before going down this road.

If required, secure a Business License. Municipalities, counties and state governments all have differing criteria and requirements for licensing churches. Err on the safe side here and simply ask area pastors whether they needed a Business License. If yes, remember most locations require annual license renewals.

File a property tax exemption with your state. This requirement varies by state with the property tax exemption customarily filed with your state's Department of Revenue. This is a specialized government practice where an understanding of some basic principles can be critical for you to remain in good standing with the state. These include:

1. The property must be wholly used for church purposes, which means the use of real and personal property owned by a church must be for religious worship or related administrative, educational, eleemosynary (eleemosynary is a legal term of art meaning supported by or dependent on charity), and social activities.

2. A loan or rental of the exempt property will not affect the property exemption if loaned or rented under the following conditions:
   a. The loan or rental must be to a nonprofit organization, association, corporation, or school;
   b. The loan or rental must be for an eleemosynary (charitable) activity;
   c. The rental income must be reasonable and devoted solely to the operation and maintenance of the property.

Some churches find creative ways to help defray ministry costs by renting out their facilities during the workweek. Many pastors appreciate the income available through a scaled down version of WeWork, a shared office workspace. But keep in mind that the income received from renting your facilities to for-profit purposes then becomes taxable income. It is called Unrelated Business Income Tax (UBIT). I would recommend you seek the services of a CPA working in the nonprofit sector to assist you in filing the required annual forms.

One last word on UBIT. When the annual revenue of a church or ministry related to for-profit facility rental purposes, grows to equal or exceed ministry/charitable giving, the IRS begins to wonder what "business" the church is really engaged in. Too much UBIT may prompt a site visit and audit from your local IRS examiners. It may even result in the loss of your property tax exemption and the 501(c)(3) charitable organization status.

3. When property is not used for church purposes, the exemption is lost. If a portion of the exempt property is used for commercial rather than church purposes, that portion must be segregated and taxed whether or not the proceeds received by the church from the commercial use are applied to church purposes.

   a. This includes the use of property to promote the business interests of individuals or for-profit organizations. Examples can be music teachers, artists, performers, photographers, travel agents and others. All of these persons can be hired for their personal services for allowable church purposes. However, if they use an exempt property (church) to further their own business, it becomes a commercial purpose.

b. This also includes a church using their charitable organization status to accept third-party donations. For instance, consider a situation where a church has agreed to become a "partner" with a for-profit firm founded and owned by one of the staff pastors (a side business). The firm conducts ministry related-work and was planning to hold a large revenue-producing event in a commercial event facility. Several affluent business people were invited to underwrite portions of the event, and the church agreed to receive the checks, provide a donation receipt, and then use those funds to pay event vendors. This type of arrangement improperly extends the church's nonprofit status to the for-profit firm and could result in multiple sanctions from both state and federal authorities.

Commercial/Business Steps

Open church bank accounts find a reputable bank in your local area and open a checking and savings account for the church. This will likely be the same financial institution offering the church a credit card so ensure you shop around for favorable rates, terms, and services. Find out about any hidden fees and explore their experience in doing business with other churches.

The bank will require the state-approved Articles of Incorporation and the EIN in order to establish these accounts. This step, therefore, follows completion of Legal steps 1 & 2 above.

A quick note on credit cards. Financial institutions issuing the credit cards normally set a limit on the cards, for instance, a limit up to $10,000. In addition to the planter's card, it is prudent to have one or two other leaders in possession of a card in order to purchase goods and services required by the church. In light of this necessity, work to establish a policy on the use of church credit cards so that church funds are spent appropriately and limits not exceeded.

Formulate a core ideology for your church plant consisting of a mission statement and shared values. For some practical application of this step, check out the public domain Harvard Business Review article by Jim Collins and Jerry Porras (see footnote).[2] The completion of this essential step will also enhance the efforts towards developing a church logo and website design.

Develop a church logo. My advice is to seek a skilled professional graphic artist type who can translate the essence of your new church plant into the logo. Yes, this will cost you some coin, but the right logo is well worth the investment. Be

---

[2] Jerry Porras and Jim Collins, "Building Your Company's Vision," *Harvard Business Review,* September-October 1996, http://www.vision4dynamics.com/f/Building_Your_Company's_Vision.pdf.

sure to ask for multiple options in the preliminary design phase so that the designer can craft what works best for you.

In addition to sharing your core ideology with the graphic artist, be prepared with answers to these questions:

1. What look and feel are we after? This may help the logo designer with color and font options.
2. What other church logos inspire you or could conceivably serve as a starting point? Be able to articulate what specifically captures your interest or the personal appeal of the logo.
3. What theme and background colors come to mind as a starting point? This is a matter of personal taste so give some thought to seeking advice from aesthetically gifted people.

Purchase website URL. The creation of your church website often occurs before the official launch. The web address is critically important and requires some research to determine if your desired web address is available.

Consult sites such as www.register.com to determine if your preferred web address is available. Most churches use the ".com" or ".org" convention. If your favorite choices are already taken, then it may require some creative options to secure a web address. Once you land an available web address, go ahead and immediately purchase it. After purchasing the URL, future steps will include finding a web designer to build your website and finding a place to host it. Go ahead and buy all other similar URLs so that you can set up a re-direct to your website to help drive traffic to the site. This will also help Google, or other search engines find your website.

Create Social Media Channels. Use of Facebook, Twitter, Instagram, LinkedIn, Snapchat, Tumblr, Google+, and other social media services to promote the church plant and connect people even before the official launch. Start a page for the church and keep it fresh and updated. Where possible, use humor, creativity, and actual photos of the developing church (not stock) to build a genuine audience. Remember, people often survey your social media before visiting. Consider starting unique hashtags to help others enjoy the process. There are also benefits to partnering with social media-savvy church members to help mobilize your message.

Management Steps

This is bonus material once the church planter completes the legal and commercial/ business steps.

Create a permanent document repository. This is the single place to retain all founding documents, important papers, policies and procedures, and minutes of your board or elder meetings. Best practices call for both electronic and paper copies. Scan and retain an electronic copy in a file entitled something like "Official Records." Purchase a two-inch three-ring binder to store paper copies and secure the binder in a safe location.

Find a reputable and experienced church bookkeeping service to set up your accounting system and to handle payroll. This is imperative if you want to avoid legal problems. Go ahead and spend the money. Remember, if errors, irregularities or violations of laws occur — you are responsible. This is the domain of those with experience, training, and preparation; it's not a place to save money. Keep in mind that a church payroll can be as complicated as most large businesses and requires specialized knowledge of little-known IRS regulations. The peculiarities of the IRS Code for ministers and churches can be staggering, so please don't engage a discounted, generic bookkeeping service to handle these matters for your church plant.

Secure insurance through a reputable broker experienced in the church sector of nonprofits. This is not optional; you need insurance. And your need for additional coverage expands alongside your attendance. We live in a litigious world, and wise stewardship requires some protection obtained through an appropriate and comprehensive insurance policy. Below are some of the types of coverage you will want to examine and discuss with a reputable broker.

1. Property — protection for leased or owned buildings, equipment, and vehicles.
2. Liability — to reduce exposure from lawsuits and claims for false accusations, accidents, negligence, or inappropriate behavior. In general, here are multiple types of coverages to include:
   a. General — when the church is legally liable for bodily injury or property damage and may include defense costs for litigation.
   b. Sexual misconduct — coverage for real incidents, allegations, and defense costs.

c. Directors and officers — coverage for decisions made by your board, officers, and trustees.

d. Employment practices — for when you have staff, to address claims arising from employment-related events like claims of discrimination, wrongful termination, etc.

e. Employee benefits — to cover claims arising from errors or omissions with regard to the benefits an employee should have received.

f. Professional liability/counseling acts — coverage arising from accusations against pastors or counselors of physical and/or emotional harm.

g. Workers compensation — depends on your state's requirements.

h. Medical payments — this endorsement allows a goodwill payment to individuals injured on church property regardless of fault.

i. Excess or umbrella — added coverage over all other liability coverage should those limits be reached through claims activity.

j. Business auto — coverage when you have church-owned vehicles.

3. Other coverages (not an exhaustive list):

a. Inland marine — refers to portable equipment moved around.

b. Business income — replaces lost or reduced income the church suffers due to damage by a covered event.

    c.   Electronic data processing — coverage for all technology and systems used by the church.

    d.   Cyber and privacy — coverage for liability for a data breach in which members' personal information is exposed or stolen through unauthorized access of the church's website, server or software.

    e.   Water, flood, earthquake — these coverages are available in areas prone to experience these events.

Finishing these tasks is an important step in the process of planting a local church. However, after moving through the pre-launch, launch, and post-launch phases, there awaits another challenge: Training others to steward these items even further than your time, ability, and focus allow.

Raising up the right deacons and elders in character and competency to continue the leadership of these areas is vital to your growing church. Your church will need to face the legal, commercial/business, and management needs such as acquiring a facility, navigating the liabilities of youth groups and mission trips, managing the human resources of a growing staff, or blossoming para-church organizations in and around your church. All these wonderful opportunities come with gospel growth, giving you more opportunities to train others to steward these matters beyond your ability and time constraints. You will bless them with real leadership and responsibility, and they will share the burden to chart the course for the future of the church as well.

CONCLUSION

Remember my sentiments in the introductory letter about the church planting adventure requiring a clear calling, great courage, strong convictions, and multiple forms of perseverance? Perhaps now after reading the pages of this book, you have a far better grasp of why these virtues are essential to church planting. I hope *Charting the Course* gives you a clear sense of how to proceed and navigate through these legal requirements to plant your local church.

I pray that you have been encouraged and equipped to move out and press forward with the new church God has called you to plant. Go and plant it — and keep this book open while you venture forward in those early days. May your obedience to your calling result in hearing years from now, "Well done, good and faithful servant!"

PRACTICES

APPENDICES

APPENDIX ONE

ARTICLES OF INCORPORATION: TYPICAL ELEMENTS FOR A CHURCH FILING

The forms and requirements for Articles (Certificate) of Incorporation are state specific. Some states delegate this function to a County Clerk while most states retain the function of incorporating nonprofit corporations at the Secretary of State level. A simple web surfing session will quickly uncover the appropriate level and official where you can apply to incorporate your church.

Most states offer online filing and completion of forms. The process of completing the Articles of Incorporation is usually quick – within a week or two from the time of the form is completed and payment made. The approving authority will mail the approved, official Articles of Incorporation to the person and address provided in the form. This founding document should be safely and securely filed in a permanent repository after a scanned electronic copy is made. (Your banker and some vendors will ask for a copy of the Articles of Incorporation.)

The most common elements of the Articles of Incorporation include the following:

- Name of the church – this is the unique corporate name of your church discussed above
- Existence – usually in perpetuity or until Jesus returns
- Effective date – the month, day, and year you want your church to be incorporated
- Members – there are typically two types for a church: corporate members (those people who will be authorized to be officers and directors) and church members (attendees who go through a membership process and plan to make your church their church home)
- Type of Non-profit – this happens to be a state specific requirement (New York in the Certificate of Incorporation example) and will require reading the instructions accompanying the online form
- Registered Agent – see Preparation point #3 above for explanation
- Principal Office – this is a street address (not a post office box) and may actually be the address of the church planter's residence at the time of incorporation. Once you have a real church office, provide the update to the issuing authority so they will mail important documents to the correct address.

- Directors – the approving authority will need the names and addresses of at least three people serving in the capacity of start-up director. (See comments under Preparation #4 for more details.)
- Purposes – it is critically important to use the language consistent with the IRS section 501(c)(3). You will be well served to copy verbatim the language provided in the Certificate of Incorporation below.)
- Prohibited Activities – Please note the inclusion of the standards for tax-exempt organizations often referred to as the "no, no, nots." Be sure to include these verbatim.
- Dissolution clause – this is similar to the Purposes clause . . . the prescribed language has great legal meaning to distinguish nonprofit corporations from for-profit ones. Copy this verbatim and you will be good to go.
- Indemnification – This is standard

Note: Several of the clauses in the Articles of Incorporation will be included in your Bylaws. This repetition isn't a problem as it is far better to protect your new church by including these legal provisions. Remember, each state will have different information requests for you to include in the Articles of Incorporation.

Sample Articles (Certificate) of Incorporation[1]

State of New York
Department of State
Division of Corporations, State Records and Uniform
Commercial Code
One Commerce Plaza, 99 Washington Ave. Albany, NY
12231

Certificate of Incorporation

Pursuant to section 402 of the Not-for-Profit Corporation law of State of New York, the undersigned majority of who are citizens of the United States do hereby submit the Certificate of Incorporation for the purpose of forming a nonprofit corporation.

ARTICLE 1:
Name

The name of the corporation is **(insert name of church here)**.

ARTICLE 2:
Existence

The corporation shall have perpetual existence.

---

[1] Another sample of Articles of Incorporation for the state of Kentucky can be found here, https://www.sos.ky.gov/bus/business-filings/Forms/Documents/AINon-Profit.PDF. Other states may have similar forms.

ARTICLE 3:
Effective Date

The effective date of incorporation shall be upon filing by the Division of Corporations.

ARTICLE 4:
Members

Section 1. Corporate Members

ABC Church shall have no corporate members. Any action, which would otherwise require approval by corporate members, shall only require approval of the Full Council of Elders (hereafter referred to as "Elders"). All rights, which would otherwise vest in the corporate members, shall vest in the Elders.

Section 2. Church Members

Nothing contained in Section 1 of this Article shall be construed to limit the right of ABC Church to refer to persons associated with the church ministry as 'members' even though such persons are not corporate members, and no such reference in or outside of these Articles or the bylaws shall constitute anyone being a corporate member. The Elders may in specific circumstances condition its approval of matters on approval by the church membership.

ARTICLE 5:
Type of non-profit corporation

The corporation is not for profit as defined in subparagraph (a)(5) of Section 102 (Definitions) of the Not-for-Profit Corporation Law and a Religious Corporation.

ARTICLE 6:
Registered Agent and Office

The Secretary of State is designated as agent of the corporation upon whom process against it may be served. The name and address to which the Secretary of State shall mail a copy of any process accepted on behalf of the corporation is:

(Insert Name)

Address 1

City, State, Zip, AND County

The name of the registered agent at this address is: **(insert name of registered agent here)**

ARTICLE 7:
Principal Office

The corporation has a principal office. The street address of the principal office is:

Address 1

Address 2

County

ARTICLE 8:
Mailing Address

Address 1
Address 2
County

ARTICLE 9:
Directors

The corporation's initial directors are as follows:
Name, Address 1, Address 2
Name, Address 1, Address 2
Name, Address 1, Address 2

ARTICLE 10:
Indemnification

The corporation does indemnify any directors, officers, employees, incorporators, and members of the corporation from any liability regarding the corporation and the affairs of the corporation, unless the person fraudulently and intentionally violated the law and/or maliciously conducted acts to damage and/or defraud the corporation, or as otherwise provided under applicable statute.

ARTICLE 11:
Purpose

- ABC Church exists to **(insert mission statement here)**.

- We will seek to accomplish our mission through various ministries including but not limited to: gathering in communal worship services, administration of the Lord's supper and baptism, intimate prayer and discussion in community groups, and other ministries and initiatives as deemed necessary by the governing body.

- The general purpose for which ABC Church is formed is to operate exclusively for such religious, charitable, and educational purposes as will qualify it as an exempt organization under section 501 (C) (3) of the Internal Revenue Code or corresponding provisions of any subsequent federal tax laws, including, for such purposes, the making of distributions to organizations which qualify as tax-exempt organizations under that code.

- ABC Church will not, as a substantial part of its activities, disseminate propaganda or otherwise attempt to influence legislation; nor shall it participate or intervene (by publication or distribution of any statements or otherwise) in any political campaign on behalf of any candidate for public office.

- No part of the net earnings of the corporation will inure to the benefit of any individual or member.

- The character and essence of the corporation are the same as the purpose.

ARTICLE 12:
Type of New York Non-Profit Corporation

The corporation shall be a type B corporation pursuant to section 201 of the Not-for-Profit corporation law.

ARTICLE 13:
Prohibited Activities

No part of the net earnings of the corporation shall inure to the benefit of, or be distributable to its members, trustees, officers, or other private persons, except that the corporation shall be authorized and empowered to pay reasonable compensation for services rendered and to make payments and distributions in furtherance of the purposes set forth in Article 11. No substantial part of the activities of the corporation shall be the carrying on of propaganda, or otherwise attempting to influence legislation, and the corporation shall not participate in, or intervene in (including the publishing or distribution of statements) any political campaign on behalf of or in opposition to any candidate for public office. Notwithstanding any other provision of these articles, this corporation shall not, except to an insubstantial degree, engage in any activities or exercise any powers that are not in furtherance of the purposes of this corporation.

ARTICLE 14:
Distributions Upon Dissolution

No person, firm or corporation shall ever receive any dividends or profits from the undertaking of this corporation and upon dissolution of this corporation all of its assets remaining after payment of all costs will go to causes furthering the gospel of the Lord Jesus Christ, in the evangelical tradition, which has qualified for exemption under Section 501 (C) (3) of the Internal Revenue Code. None of the assets will be distributed to any member or officer of this corporation.

ARTICLE 15:
Incorporator

The name and address of the Incorporator is: **(insert name and full mailing address here)**.

I, the undersigned, for the purpose of forming a New York non-profit corporation under the laws of the State of New York, do make, file and record this Certificate, and do certify that the facts herein states are true.

_____

Signature

_____

Date

APPENDIX TWO

FEDERAL EMPLOYER IDENTIFICATION NUMBER FORM & INSTRUCTIONS

The SS-4 Application for Employer Identification Number can easily be completed online and submitted to the IRS . . . at no cost. The Federal Employer Identification Number (FEIN) is simply an identification number for tax, banking, and credit purposes. It's like a personal social security number – your church will use this number mostly for commercial purposes like opening checking and savings accounts, establishing credit, to file pertinent tax and informational returns (if or when required).

The FEIN is needed first so apply for it online. Be sure to retain the approved form with your number in a secure place.

The FEIN is not a tax-exempt number. Tax-exemption involves other IRS and state government agencies.

This is the link to apply online for the FIN (IRS Form SS-4 and Instructions:

https://www.irs.gov/businesses/small-businesses-
   self-employed/apply-for-an-employer-
   identification-number-ein-online

Here are a few quick tips for filling out the form:[1]

- Line 1 – the legal, unique name of your church as
  we have discussed before
- Line 2 – usually "NA"
- Line 3 – same as Line 2
- Line 4b – skip if you are registering in your home
  state within the U.S.
- Line 7a – you are the responsible party
- Line 8a – type "x" in the "No" box and skip 8b and
  8c
- Line 9a – remember to check "church or church-
  controlled organization"
- Line 9b – skip
- Line 10 – right response is "Started new business"
  and type in "church"
- Line 11 – see instructions
- Line 12 – means the last month of the fiscal year
  you have chosen (usually June or December)
- Line 13 - employees anticipated would be listed as
  "Other" so enter a "1–2"
- Line 14 – do not check the box
- Line 16 – check "Other" and type in Church" on
  that line

---

[1] Note that I am not addressing every single line on the form as many
are self-explanatory.

- Line 17 – enter "Church – to be operated exclusively for religious, charitable and educational purposes"

APPENDIX THREE

BYLAWS "MUST HAVES"

Bylaws are required by states as part of the process of incorporation. This is a corporate, founding document that clearly lays out the structure, principles, major processes in which an organization governs itself. If a church desires a tax-exempt letter of recognition from the IRS and completes Form 1023, the IRS will also have a copy of your bylaws. This can be a double-edged sword, as the version of the bylaws they have likely will be outdated due to subsequent revisions over time – and usually most churches do not send in bylaw revisions to governmental agencies. The bylaws' version the IRS has in hand becomes the "official" document for their purposes. Kind of scary, huh?

The Information or Digital Age in which we live operates at a far faster and dynamic pace than at any time in history. This is true in all facets of life – societally, legally, financially, educationally, etc. In the past decade, a small but growing number of attorneys operating in the nonprofit space (and especially in the church specialty) have rethought some of the more traditional approaches for preparing bylaws. The rationale – laws, the interpretation of laws in court cases, regulations, and societal norms are changing so fast that bylaws often need to adjust accordingly.

While the basic legal requirements need to be met in the bylaws, some of the bylaw facets more prone to frequent update and revision could be documented in a linked document. This "linked" document frequently is labeled something like, "The Written Doctrines" or the "Philosophy of Ministry". You can see examples of how this "linkage" can be accomplished in Appendix 4. If you opt to use this approach, then ensure you prepare the appropriate sections for all "linked" items" in your Philosophy of Ministry.

The table below outlines the various facets of bylaws for most states. It depicts the new "minimalistic" option alongside the traditional method of preparing bylaws.

	Minimalistic	**Traditional**
Description	· Provides the essential and required elements required under the law · Categorizes elements into primary and secondary matters · Links and moves secondary matters into a subordinate organizational document sometimes referred to as the "Philosophy of Ministry"	· Covers all required elements required under the law · Inclusive – all elements addressed in the bylaws · Statement of Faith, Beliefs & major doctrines usually included
Pros	· Usually shorter in length	· Comprehensive, with greater specificity

	· Easier for church to meet and comply with which minimizes possible legal exposure in the future · Reduces need for frequent bylaws revisions – saves senior leadership agenda time · Championed by leading Christian attorneys working in this specialized field · Lower legal costs	· Most common method used in the past – the "traditional way" · Preferred by most attorneys in the field (because this has been the normal past practice and opportunity for higher fee payments for initial prep and more frequent revisions) · Easier to find multiple examples – most older & established churches have this version
Cons	· May be perceived as placing too much trust on governing body as many areas are deliberately ambiguous and cast at a higher conceptual level · Establishment and administration required for Philosophy of Ministry · Fewer examples and templates available	· Higher legal costs due to more frequent revisions and amendments · Longer in length · Greater specificity raises the bar for church to meet and comply with provisions · Higher legal risk exposure if church is out of compliance · More senior leadership agenda time consumed by bylaws updates
Key Elements *	1. The name of the church 2. The purposes of the church	Same as Minimalistic and the following: 1. Statement of Faith

3. Prohibited activities clause 4. Definition of the governing body 5. Qualifications, selection, and expulsion of corporate members (usually elders/deacons) 6. Time and place of annual business meetings 7. Designation of the fiscal year 8. The calling of special business meetings 9. Notice for annual and special meetings 10. Quorums at meetings of the membership and church governing board 11. Filling of vacancies on the church governing board 12. Voting rights and requirements 13. Selection, tenure, and removal of officers and directors 14. Responsibilities of directors and officers 15. The procedure for amending bylaws 16. The procedure and voting requirements for purchases and	2. Ecclesiastical authority of pastors/elders 3. Mutual interest clause (establishment of a code of conduct for staff, volunteers, members, and any partners of the church) 4. Licensing and ordination requirements 5. Church membership roles & responsibilities 6. Church member discipline and care 7. Eldership & deaconship processes **Note:** If a church planter opts to use the Minimalistic approach, these elements would then need to be mentioned in the bylaws and thus "linked" to the Philosophy of Ministry or The Written Doctrines document. The topics and narratives contained in the Philosophy of Written Doctrines then can be updated and revised without the somewhat arduous and difficult

	conveyances of church property 17. The designation of standing committees (such as audit committee, an investment committee, and an insurance committee) 18. Clause to resolve disputes through mediation or arbitration 19. Indemnification 20. Keeping of books & records	process of amending the bylaws.

* Adapted from the *Model Nonprofit Corporations Act (3rd ed. 2008)*. Source: Church Law & Tax, June 25, 2015, *What are Church Bylaws* by Richard Hammar.

APPENDIX FOUR

SAMPLE BYLAWS

Please make use of the following sample bylaws, but first note these caveats:

1. The use of templates or examples may be useful to prepare a first draft. It can save time and considerable legal fees, *BUT* ... (see the next caveat.)

2. Each state determines the required elements for bylaws of nonprofit organizations. We highly recommend employing an attorney licensed in your state and experienced in the church sector to at least review your bylaws before your bylaws are approved and ratified.

3. Poorly drafted and constructed bylaws are a train wreck waiting to happen. It may be an open door for the planter to start a prison ministry from the inside.

4.   The following contains articles, clauses, and language represent a composite set of bylaws adapted from multiple, existing churches for the purpose of illustrating and reinforcing the teaching points of this book. The Minimalistic approach is presented using the plurality of elders governance model.

BYLAWS

XYZ Church

prepared _____, approved _____

PREAMBLE

These Bylaws govern the affairs of XYZ Church, a religious non-profit corporation. XYZ is organized under the _____ State Not-for- Profit Corporation Law (NPCL), as amended (the "Law").

ARTICLE 1:
Name

1.1. The name of this corporation (hereinafter also referred to as "church," "this church," "the church," or "XYZ") is XYZ Church, of (<u>City</u>), (<u>County</u>) and State of _____.

ARTICLE 2:
Purpose

2.1. XYZ is formed for any lawful purpose or purposes not expressly prohibited under the Law. It is organized and shall be operated exclusively for religious, charitable and educational purposes within the meaning of Section 501(c)(3) of the Internal Revenue Code, as amended (the "Internal Revenue Code"). The church's purposes also include limited participation in any other activities, including taxable activities, but only to the extent the activities would be permitted by a tax-exempt organization.

2.2. More particularly, but without limitation, the purposes of XYZ are to:

(a) Encourage and promote the advancing of the gospel of Jesus Christ.

(b) Establish and maintain the worship of God.

(c) Provide a basis of relationship and community among fellow believers.

(d) Encourage and promote the spiritual growth and discipleship of believers.

(e) License and oversee ministers of the gospel.

(f) Respond to human need with ministries of service and compassion.

(g) Own, hold in trust, use, sell, convey, mortgage, lease, or otherwise acquire or dispose of such property (real or chattel) as may be needed for accomplishing the mission of the church.

ARTICLE 3:
Statement of Faith

3.1 XYZ Church's Statement of Faith is presented in the Philosophy of Ministry Document.

ARTICLE 4:
Authority, Government, and Affiliations

4.1. XYZ is a self-governing body, autonomous from all other church bodies and independent of denominational control. XYZ may voluntarily affiliate with other churches of like faith and practice.

4.2. XYZ is first and foremost an ecclesiastical body of believers, with Christ as its head. Christ delegates his authority to elders in each local church; they care for his church and are accountable to him for the use or abuse of that authority.

4.3. The Bible is the supreme governing document. The Bible is the final authority for all questions of theology and ethics, including (but not limited to) sexual identity and sexual practice. The elders of the church have the final authority for the interpretation of the pertinent biblical texts on the aforementioned topics.

4.4. XYZ is secondarily a civil corporation, the governance of which is established by its Articles of Incorporation and these Bylaws. The Articles of Incorporation and these Bylaws, however, are subordinate to the Bible and must be interpreted in light of the Scriptures. The Bylaws establish the ecclesiastical bodies that govern XYZ. The powers, duties and function of the body shall be presumed to be ecclesiastical unless explicitly required for civil purposes.

4.5. The form of government for this church shall be elder-led and congregational affirmation.

ARTICLE 5:
Board of Elders

5.1 XYZ is governed by a Board of Directors (henceforth referred to as the "Board of Elders" or "BOE"). The BOE shall have the power to determine all issues regarding the Church, having all of the rights, powers and responsibilities of a board of directors pursuant to the Internal Revenue Code, subject to any limitations under the Internal Revenue

Code, the Articles of Incorporation of the Church, and these Bylaws.

5.2 The minimum number of elders shall be a plurality of three. There is no maximum number.

5.3 All elders shall be members of the BOE for the purposes of the Law.

5.4 During the next two years of XYZ's existence, a temporary Council of Advisors shall be appointed to guide, advise and provide counsel to the Senior Elder until such a time as two other qualified elders are in place at XYZ. Once XYZ has three elders ordained per Article 6, this temporary Council of Advisors will be dissolved and XYZ will be governed in accordance with Articles 5 and 7.

ARTICLE 6:
Qualifications, Selections, and Service of Elders

6.1 To be considered as an elder, a man must have been called by God into leadership at XYZ (Acts 20:28), exhibit the highest Christian character, demonstrate the requisite competencies of pastoral ministry, and display unity with the other elders, according to the qualifications of Scripture (1 Timothy 3:1–7; Titus 1:5–9).

Calling: an elder possesses a godly ambition to serve in the office of elder. This aspiration comes from the Holy Spirit, who establishes leaders in the church (Acts 20:28). This internal sense of divine calling must be confirmed by the elders and members of XYZ.

Character: an elder exhibits the character qualities as detailed in 1 Timothy 3:1–7 and Titus 1:5–9. These qualities include being above approach, a mature Christian, a good husband (if married) and a good father (if he has children), temperate, self-controlled, without addictions, respectable and respected by others, and gentle and kind rather than contentious. While still sinful and needing to repent of sin when his life does not manifest these qualities, an elder must exhibit these characteristics in increasing measure.

Competencies: an elder demonstrates the requisite competencies for this office, including the ability to teach (cherishes sound doctrine for himself, is able to communicate sound doctrine to others, and is able to refute false doctrine), lead (carry out governing responsibilities), pray (for all church matters, especially for the sick), and shepherd (exercise church discipline, protect the members, and provide stellar examples of faithfulness and obedience for members to follow).

Chemistry: an elder displays good chemistry with his fellow elders so that they are united in theological vision, core values, philosophy of ministry, and brotherhood.

6.2 Elders Selection - To be selected as an elder, the following process is generally followed: assessment of calling, character, competencies, and chemistry; successful completion of the elder-in-training process; approval by his local elders and by the Board of Elders; affirmation by the members; and installation as an elder. In the case of hiring an elder from outside of XYZ, the investigation, interviews, and due diligence carried out by the elders doing the hiring constitutes the above process. Upon his hiring, he is installed as an elder.

6.3 Elder must whole-heartedly affirm the Statement of Faith, Bylaws, and other important documents of XYZ. They agree to notify the BOE if they take "exception" to anything in these documents, and the board will determine if their exceptions are disqualifying.

6.4 Elder Service - may be vocational or bi-vocational, paid or unpaid. Elder service continues for as long as an elder is qualified to be an elder. Sabbaticals for various reasons may be granted for a season, during which the elder is inactive and does not vote. Resignation from the office of elder must be preceded by a letter of resignation, to be approved by the Board of Elders.

6.5 An elder shall be dismissed from office in the following instances (an illustrative, not exhaustive, list): moral impropriety, doctrinal error, bringing reproach to the name of Christ and/or XYZ, incompetency, disunity with the rest of the elders, and any other failure that would fall under the category of actions that demand church discipline. A task force established by the Board of Elders shall investigate a credible charge against an elder, and shall follow the investigative process outlined in the Philosophy of Ministry Document.

6.6 Service as an elder confers the authority to preach, oversee the administration of the ordinances, marry, and enjoy all the rights and privileges accorded to licensed or ordained ministers under state law.

ARTICLE 7:
Roles and Responsibilities of Elders

7.1 Elders of XYZ commit by the grace of God to intentionally and responsibly fulfill the biblical duties and responsibilities of Christ's under-shepherds. These include, but are not limited to, the following:

(a) Rule/lead the church (1 Timothy 3:4–5; 5:17). The elders are responsible to oversee all the ministries and business affairs of the church.

(b) Preach and teach the Bible (1 Timothy 4:13; 5:17; 2 Timothy 3:16–4:2), submitting to the final authority of the scriptures in all matters (Psalm 119:1–176; 2 Timothy 3:16–4:2; 2 Peter 1:19–21).

(c) Instruct, instruct and encourage the church with sound doctrine (Ephesians 4:11–14, 1 Thessalonians 5:12; Titus 1:9) and protect the church from false doctrine (Acts 20:28–31; Titus 1:9). (d) Give devoted attention to prayer and Scripture study (Acts 6:4).

(e) Care for and watch over the souls of the people in the church (1 Peter 5:2–5, Hebrews 13:17).

(f) Pray for the church and those who are sick (Acts 6:4; James 5:14).

(g) Handle and distribute money to the glory of God (Acts 11:29–30; 1 Timothy 3:2; 1 Peter 5:2). This includes stewarding of church finances and property using generally accepted accounting practices. It includes making wise property purchases, prudent decisions about the proper investment of church assets, and overseeing the salary and benefit structures for church employees, etc. It also includes giving generously to the church from personal income.

(h) Develop Godly leadership in the church (Acts 14:23; 1 Timothy 3:10; 4:14; 5:22; Titus 1:5). This includes small group leaders and deacons, both of whom are under the oversight of the elders.

(i) Lovingly discipline members who persist in sin, with the goal of restoration to full fellowship (Matthew 18:15–20; Galatians 6:1; Titus 3:10).

(j) Protect the church from divisiveness (Titus 3:10).

7.2 Elders may alter, amend, or repeal and adopt new Articles of Incorporation, Bylaws, or Statement of Faith.

7.3 Governance - The Board of Elders may structure and organize itself however it deems necessary for the sake of simplicity, clarity of communication, and efficiency of organization, according to the needs of the Church and the size of the BOE. Any such restructuring must preserve the plurality of elders and the calling, character, competencies, and chemistry requirements for elders articulated above.

7.4 To promote efficient handling of its matters, the BOE may appoint various councils and committees from within its membership, the staff, and from the church at large. These councils and committees shall perform tasks solely in accordance with the duties and with powers specifically delegated by the BOE.

7.5 All councils and committees shall exist for the period specified by the BOE and serve under its authority.

ARTICLE 8:
Board of Elders' Meeting

8.1 The BOE shall hold regular meetings.

8.2 Additional special meetings may be called by either the chairman of the elders or by a majority of the elders.

8.3 A selected member of the elders or staff shall make a reasonable effort to notify the team of elders of any special meetings. Notice of regular meetings need not be given.

8.4 Members of the BOE may participate in a meeting of the Board by means of a conference telephone, video technology, or similar communications equipment by means of which all persons participating in the meeting can hear each other at the same time. Participation by such means shall constitute presence in person at a meeting.

8.5 Each elder shall have one vote.

8.6 As pertains to major issues,[1] the BOE shall try to act by consensus. However, a 75% majority of the Board present and voting at a meeting at which a quorum is present shall be sufficient to constitute an act of the Board, unless (a) the act of a greater number is required by the Act, the Articles of Incorporation or these Bylaws, or (b) there is a simple majority with only a single dissenting vote, in which case a number lower than 75% is sufficient. A member of the Board who is present at a meeting and abstains from a vote is considered to be present and voting for the purpose of determining the decision of the Board.

8.7 Fifty-one percent (51%) of the number of individuals serving on the BOE shall constitute a quorum for the transaction of business at any meeting of the BOE. The members of the board present at a duly called or held meeting at which a quorum is present may continue to transact business even if enough members of the BOE leave the

---

[1] "Major Issue" means subjects like, but not limited to, church discipline, major purchases, the selection of a Lead Pastor, the addition of new elders, etc.

meeting so that less than a quorum remains. However, no action may be approved without the vote of at least a majority of the number of members of the BOE in attendance required to constitute a quorum. If a quorum is present at no time during a meeting, a majority of the members of the BOE may adjourn and reconvene the meeting one time without further notice.

8.8 The BOE shall keep a record of its proceedings.

8.9 Any action required or permitted to be taken by the BOE may be taken without a meeting if all of the members of the BOE, individually or collectively, consent in writing or via electronic transmission to the action. Such action by written consent or consents shall be filed with the minutes.

8.10 Non-elders, including officers, may be present and have a voice at BOE meetings at the discretion of the elders, but they will not have a vote.

ARTICLE 9:
Senior Elder (Lead Pastor)

9.1 The BOE determines the "senior elder," who functions as the first among equals and is the Lead Pastor for the church. It is the duty of the lead pastor to help lead the eldership and the rest of the church in effectively obeying God's leading as revealed in Scripture.

9.2 The Lead Pastor shall be called for an indefinite term of office.

9.3 The primary responsibility of the Lead Pastor shall be preaching, casting vision, leadership development, administration and oversight of the elders, and oversight of the BOE meetings. He shall be directly accountable to the elders, who will advise, assist, and evaluate both he and his work.

9.4 The Lead Pastor shall serve as the President of the Corporation.

9.5 In addition to the stipulations of Article 6, the Lead Pastor shall be terminated when or if he fails to meet the moral and spiritual qualifications for office, is otherwise injurious to the church, negligent in the performance of his duties, or unable to fulfill his responsibilities due to age or sickness.

9.6 The Lead Pastor may not be removed from his position unless a 100% quorum of at least three-fourths of the elders (excluding himself) vote for his termination. As a matter of due diligence, the elders will also call a meeting of the small group leaders and seek their advice. They also may seek the advice of other trusted pastors.

9.7 Where appropriate, the BOE shall be gracious in the determination of the timing and amount of severance pay.

9.8 If a vacancy is created as a result of the resignation, death or removal of the Lead Pastor, the vacancy shall be filled as soon as practical.

9.9 In the event that a new Lead Pastor is to be called, the Pastoral Search Committee will be made up of the elders.

9.10 When the elders identify a candidate for the senior pastor position, the elders will present him to the XYZ' membership for affirmation. The elders will conscientiously listen to any objections from members of the congregation. They will discuss them at a subsequent BOE meeting.

9.11 Should the elders appoint an interim pastor, he also will meet the qualifications for elders outlined in Article 6.

ARTICLE 10:
Officers

10.1 The elders shall designate the following state-required officers:

(a) a President, who is also the Chairman and Lead Pastor.

(b) a Secretary of the corporation from the active church membership.

(c) a Treasurer of the corporation from the active church membership.

10.2 The BOE may also choose other officers and agents as it deems necessary. Any number of offices may be held by the same person, except that the office of president and secretary may not be held by the same person.

10.3 All officers are to function in line with the Statement of Faith, Core Values, and Mission Statement of this church.

10.4 The President.

(a) The office of President is filled by the Lead Pastor of the church.

(b) The President shall be the presiding officer for XYZ and shall, subject to the provisions of these Bylaws, (i) have general and active management of the affairs of XYZ and have general supervision of its officers, agents and employees; (ii) preside at all meetings of the BOE; and (iii) perform those other duties incident to the office of president and as from time to time may be assigned to him by the BOE.

(c) The President's term is indefinite.

(d) The President shall chair an annual XYZ member's business meeting that includes a report of the financial state of the church.

10.5 The Secretary

(a) The Secretary of the Corporation shall be selected annually from among the active XYZ membership during the first meeting of the year. The term of office shall be for one year, and he/she may succeed themselves.

(b) The Secretary shall keep a true and accurate record of all meetings of the church and the BOE. He/she may personally fulfill the duties or delegate as agreed to by the BOE.

(c) The Secretary shall be custodian of all legal documents and shall be authorized to sign all official and legal documents, to conduct church correspondence where required, and to perform any other functions as are customary or as may be directed by the BOE.

10.6 The Treasurer

(a) The Treasurer of the Corporation shall be selected annually from among the active XYZ membership during the first meeting of the year. The term of office shall be for one year, and he/she may succeed themselves.

(b) The Treasurer's duties may be delegated to a bookkeeper or accountant, and shall include being the overseer and custodian of all church funds, which shall be deposited into bank accounts as, designated by the BOE.

(c) The Treasurer shall be authorized to sign checks and make disposition of funds as may be required in the accurate conduct of church business under the supervision of the BOE and consistent with this or any other provision of these Bylaws.

(d) The Treasurer, or a designee, shall give a financial report to the BOE at its regular meeting and help prepare reports that may be given to the church.

(e) The Treasurer shall perform any other functions that may be customary or as may be directed by the church or the BOE.

(f) The BOE may delegate all the duties of the Treasurer to others following consultation and consensus.

10.7 Removal of officers for good and sufficient cause shall be by action of the BOE, and reported to the congregation. No officer shall be removed from office until positive effort has been made to assist that officer in correcting the problem, except in the case of gross moral, civil or criminal misconduct, in which case removal will be immediate.

10.8 Resignations of officers shall be in writing to the President, effective on the date specified in the resignation or as determined by the BOE. (The resignation of the President shall be in writing to the BOE.)

ARTICLE 11:
Licensure and Ordination

11.1 Licensure: Any male member who in the judgment of the BOE fulfills the requirements of a deacon or elder and is called of God to the work of ministry may be granted permission for licensing according to the terms of the state, Licensing shall be ongoing until cancelled by the BOE.

11.2 Ordination: The church shall have authority to ordain any of its members who give evidence of divine call to ministry. Ordination is considered to be for life, unless there is good cause to terminate an ordination.

(a) An elder-in-waiting will be ordained at an ordination service and commissioned as an elder after he (a) meets the requirements for elder as defined in Article 4 and (b) has been an elder-in-waiting for at least 6 months.

(b) Members who become ordained shall in most cases have been licensed for at least one year or have successfully completed a Bible School education or its equivalent, as determined by the BOE. The time and place of the ordination service shall be determined by the BOE.

(c) In the case of the Lead Pastor, ordination is automatic as soon as he takes office; a ceremony may or may not be held, as determined by the BOE.

ARTICLE 12:
Deacons

12.1 The Church shall have a spiritual office of deacon that is subordinate to the office of elder. Deacons may be male or female and must meet the qualifications of a deacon set forth in the Bible (1 Timothy 3:8–13).

12.2 The general responsibility of deacons shall be to assist the elders in the ministry of XYZ. Specific responsibilities, tasks, or ministries may be given to deacons by the elders.

12.3 Scripture does not require deacons to be able to teach, indicating that their ministry is oriented in directions of mercy, service, and administration, rather than ruling through teaching. This office provides wide latitude to promote the work of ministry in and through the church in a way that involves many members in weighty and meaningful ways while protecting the elders from becoming overwhelmed with the many needs of the flock.

12.4 Deacons must whole-heartedly affirm the Bylaws, Mission Statement, Membership Agreement, Core Values, and other important documents of XYZ. They agree to notify the BOE if they take "exception" to anything in these documents. If they take exception to anything in these documents, the BOE will determine if their exceptions are disqualifying.

12.5 The process by which an individual becomes a XYZ deacon shall be established and may be amended from time to time, by the BOE.

12.6 The term of service as a deacon depends upon the commission given by the elder nominating the individual to serve as a deacon. Some deacons may serve for a specific task; others serve indefinitely.

12.7 A deacon may resign by delivering notice to the BOE or Lead Pastor, or, if due to a legitimate need, seek an extended Sabbath as determined by the BOE or Lead Pastor.

12.8 A deacon may be removed by the BOE or the lead pastor with or without cause.

ARTICLE 13:
Hired Staff

13.1 XYZ intends to hire full and part-time staff members in order to carry out its purposes. The Philosophy of Ministry Document outlines further details.

ARTICLE 14:
Church Membership

14.1. Church Members for State Law Purposes. As stated in these bylaws, the term "member" is a spiritual and theological term for a member of the body of Christ that does not have any civil effect for purposes of state law. Consistent with the biblical concept of member and this Section 14.1, members shall not have voting rights. A further description on members is found in the Philosophy of Ministry Document.

ARTICLE 15:
Member Meetings

15.1 XYZ shall meet regularly for the purpose of worship, fellowship, and mutual encouragement.

15.2 The ordinances of Baptism and the Lord's Supper shall be observed on a regular basis.

15.3 The annual meeting of the church shall be no later than May.

15.4 Special Membership Meetings may be called at any time at the request of the elders.

ARTICLE 16:
Church Discipline

16.1 God involves his church in every aspect of his redemptive work. This holds true even when God disciplines his children out of his love for them so they can share in his holiness (Heb. 12:4–11). In what is commonly referred to as church discipline, God invites his church to participate with him as he carries out his loving, redeeming discipline. God carries out his discipline in and through the body of Christ (Matt. 18:15–20). Church discipline makes membership meaningful—members and leaders care about one another and commit to encourage each other to follow Christ, enabling the church to enjoy life with God and participate in his mission.

16.2 Purpose - Church discipline has four broad purposes: (1) restoring relationships, (2) removing wickedness, (3) renewing God's people and (4) revealing God's love and glory.

16.3 People - Church discipline involves members and regular attendees who refuse to seek and obey God as well as those who seek to encourage them to turn back to Jesus Christ for mercy and forgiveness (Isa. 55:1–7). God's discipline is accomplished as the people of God seek to fight the good fight of faith together as a community of believers (1 Tim. 6:12). The elders oversee church discipline as they seek to shepherd the church.

16.4 Process - Jesus offers a general process for church discipline in Matthew 18:15–20. God's discipline expands (involving more people, to include elders) and escalates (involving increasing efforts of warnings, telling the church and removal). As agreed to in the church covenant, if a person is the subject of pending disciplinary action, the person consents and submits to the elders' continuing authority to complete the disciplinary process and not withdraw from membership. See the Philosophy of Ministry Document for more details on church discipline.

16.5 Waiver of rights - By joining this church, all members agree that the church discipline process shall provide the sole remedy for any dispute arising against the church and its agents, and they waive their right to file any legal action against the church in a civil court or agency.

ARTICLE 17:
Prohibited Activities

17.1 This church is prohibited from engaging in activities which violate its written doctrines.

17.2 This church is also prohibited from condoning, promoting, or allowing any of its assets to be used for activities that violate its written doctrines.

ARTICLE 18:
Mutual Interest

18.1 The behavior of anyone in fellowship with this church is of common interest to the Board of Elders and members. (Galatians 6:1).

18.2 This church requires every Board of Elders member, elder, deacon, staff member, and church member to adhere to a lifestyle that is consistent with the doctrines of the church as taught in the Bible.

18.3 Therefore, this church reserves the right to refuse service to any individual, whether a member or not, that is not submitting their lifestyle to this scriptural mode of conduct. This refusal would include services, benefits, and any use of church assets.

ARTICLE 19:
Dissolution

19.1 XYZ may be dissolved by a three-fourths' majority vote of the elders of the church. The quorum required is 100%.

19.2 In the event of dissolution, all outstanding debts will be retired, including any severance of current employee(s) granted by the elders. The remaining church property (or properties), both real and personal, and all proceeds therefrom, shall be given without cost to one or more likeminded churches and/or non-denominational, evangelical, or tax-exempt religious organizations. The elders shall choose the recipients.

ARTICLE 20:
Indemnification

20.1 XYZ has the power to indemnify (including the power to advance expenses to) its elders, officers, employees, and agents made a party to a proceeding, provided, however, that no such indemnity shall indemnify any such elder, officer, employee, or agent from or on account of:

(a) Acts or omissions of such elder, officer, employee, or agent finally adjudged to be intentional misconduct or a knowing violation of law.

(b) Conduct of the elder, officer, employee, or agent finally adjudged to be in violation of (identify state code here).

(c) Any transaction with respect to which it was finally adjudged that such elder, officer, employee, or agent personally received a benefit in money, property, or services to which such person was not legally entitled.

20.2 XYZ may purchase and maintain insurance, at its expense, to protect itself and any elder, officer, employee, or agent or any person who, while as an elder, officer, employee or agent of XYZ, is or was a director, officer, partner, trustee, employee or agent of another corporation, partnership, joint venture, trust, employee benefit plan or other enterprise against any expense, liability or loss, whether or not XYZ would have the power to indemnify such person against such expense, liability or loss under (your state's nonprofit act).

20.3 Any repeal or modification of this Article shall not adversely affect any right of any person existing at the time of such repeal or modification.

20.4 If any provision of this Article or any application thereof shall be invalid, unenforceable, or contrary to applicable law, the remainder of this Article, or the application of such provision to persons or circumstances other than those as to which it is held invalid, unenforceable or contrary to applicable law, shall not be affected thereby and shall continue in full force and effect.

ARTICLE 21:
Amendments

21.1 XYZ' Bylaws may be altered, amended, or repealed by the affirmative vote of a 100% quorum of at least three-fourths of the elders.

ARTICLE 22:
Books and Records

22.1 XYZ shall keep correct and complete books and records of account.

(a) Articles of Incorporation and Bylaws shall be kept indefinitely.

(b) Lists of members, elders, and officers shall be kept current.

(c) Minutes shall be kept for a minimum of 3 years.

(d) Complete financial books, records of account, and legal documents shall be maintained for such a length of time as deemed appropriate by the BOE.

22.2 Records shall be available to be inspected by any active member for reasonable purposes at any reasonable time. Requests to view records must be made to the BOE.

ACKNOWLEDGMENTS

To my wife, Patty, for the time and space to write this book. Thank you for your love and constant companionship throughout the sixteen moves around the U.S. during our forty-five years of marriage. You wisely knew I needed to learn the hard lessons of organization, leadership, and management in various sectors and industries.

To Gregg Allison for the encouragement to "just start writing," for our friendship; and for your inspirational life.

To Bill Simmonds for envisioning what consulting could look like while we waited for the wind to kite-board on the beaches of Mexico.

To Mark Driscoll and Daniel Montgomery for hiring me to serve as your executive pastor. These opportunities opened doors beyond my imagination, and I will be forever grateful.

To Dave Harvey and Justin Karl for multiple editorial and content reviews. This book would not exist without their marvelous workmanship and skill. These men "wowed" me throughout the project!

ABOUT THE AUTHOR

Tim is the former executive pastor of Sojourn Community Church, a multi-site church in the Louisville, KY area. Previously, he served as the executive pastor of Mars Hill Church in Seattle from 2007 to 2010 helping grow the church from three to twelve campuses across four states during that span.

With 25 years experience in the US Coast Guard (retiring as an O–6) and earning an MBA from Arizona State University, Tim is the founder and principal of 10 Talents Consulting. He continues to pastor at Summit Church in Fort Myers, Florida overseeing Strategic Initiatives and serve on the Sojourn Network Board of Directors.

Tim has been married to his wife Patty for 45 years and is the father of two adult children and two grandsons, who love the Lord.

ABOUT SOJOURN NETWORK

Throughout the pages of the New Testament, and especially in the book of Acts, we observe a pattern: men and women, through prayer and dependence of God and empowered by the Spirit, are sent by God (often through suffering) to spread the Word of the Lord. As this great news of new life in Christ spread into the neighboring cities, regions, provinces, and countries, gatherings of new believers formed into local communities called churches. As these gatherings formed by the thousands in the first century, the early church – taking its cue from the Scriptures — raised up qualified, called, and competent men to lead and shepherd these new congregations.

Two-thousand years later, God is still multiplying his gospel in and through his church, and the Good Shepherd is still using pastors to lead and shepherd God's people. In Sojourn Network, we desire to play our part in helping these pastors plant, grow, and multiply healthy churches.

We realize that only the Spirit can stir people's hearts and bring them into community with other believers in Jesus. Yet, by offering the pastors in our network a strong vision of planting, growing, and multiplying healthy churches and by providing them with thorough leadership assessment, funding for new churches and staff, coaching, training, renewal, and resources, we can best steward their gifts for the benefit and renewal of their local congregations.

Since 2011, our aim at Sojourn Network has been to provide the care and support necessary for our pastors to lead their churches with strength and joy — and to finish ministry well.

OTHER "HOW-TO" BOOKS

Here are the current books in the "How-To" series. Stay tuned for more.

Healthy Plurality = Durable Church: "How-To" Build and Maintain a Healthy Plurality of Elders by Dave Harvey

Life-Giving-Groups: "How-To" Grow Healthy, Multiplying Community Groups by Jeremy Linneman

Charting the Course: "How-To" Navigate the Legal Side of a Church Plant by Tim Beltz

Redemptive Participation: A "How-To" Guide for Pastors in Culture by Mike Cosper

Filling Blank Spaces: "How-To" Work with Visual Artists in Your Church by Michael Winters

Before the Lord, Before the Church: "How-To" Plan a Child Dedication Service by Jared Kennedy with Megan Kennedy

Sabbaticals: "How-To" Take a Break from Ministry before Ministry Breaks You by Rusty McKie

Leaders through Relationship: "How-To" Develop Leaders in the Local Church by Kevin Galloway

Raising the Dust: "How-To" Equip Deacons to Serve the Church by Gregg Allison & Ryan Welsh (forthcoming)

Healthy Plurality = Durable Church: "How-To" Build and Maintain a Healthy Plurality of Elders by Dave Harvey

Have you ever wondered what separates a healthy church from an unhealthy church when they have the same doctrine (and even methods) on paper? The long-term health and durability of a church simply cannot exceed the health of her elders who lead, teach, shepherd, and pray the church forward. Therefore, building and maintaining a healthy plurality of elders is the key to durability. Yet a healthy plurality is a delicate thing working through hardship and the difficulties of relationship while pursuing the noble task of eldership. If you wish to grow deeper in your theology of eldership to lead with a healthy, biblical vision of plurality, then this is your "How-To" guide.

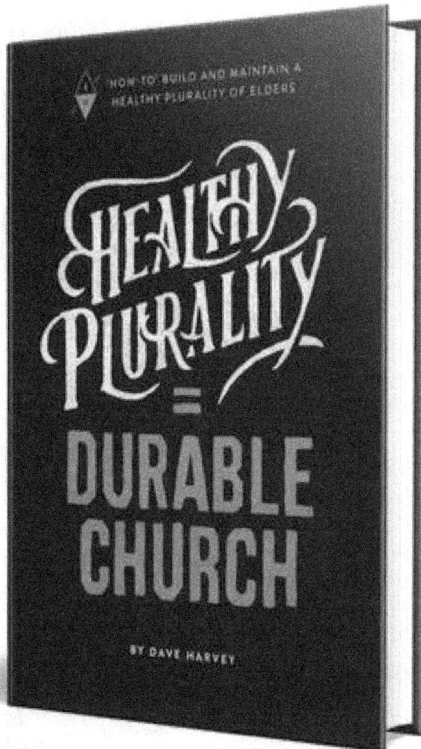

Life-Giving-Groups: "How-To" Grow Healthy, Multiplying Community Groups by Jeremy Linneman

Cultivate life-giving, Christ-centered communities. After many years of leading small groups and coaching hundreds of small group leaders, pastor and writer Jeremy Linneman has come to a bold conviction: Community groups are the best place for us — as relational beings — to become mature followers of Christ. This short book seeks to answer two questions: How can our community groups cultivate mature disciples of Christ? And how can our groups grow and multiply to sustain a healthy church? Whether you are new to community groups or tired from years of challenging ministry, *Life-Giving Groups* is a fresh, practical invitation to life together in Christ.

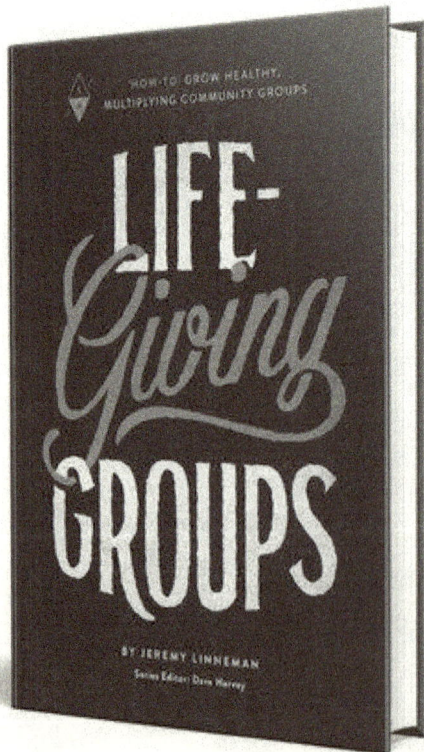

Charting the Course: "How-To" Navigate the Legal Side of a Church Plant by Tim Beltz

Planting a church? It's time to plot the course toward legal validity. Church planting is overwhelming enough before dealing with the legal and business regulations of founding a church. *Charting the Course* is for anyone, at any experience level to learn how to navigate the legal side of planting a church.

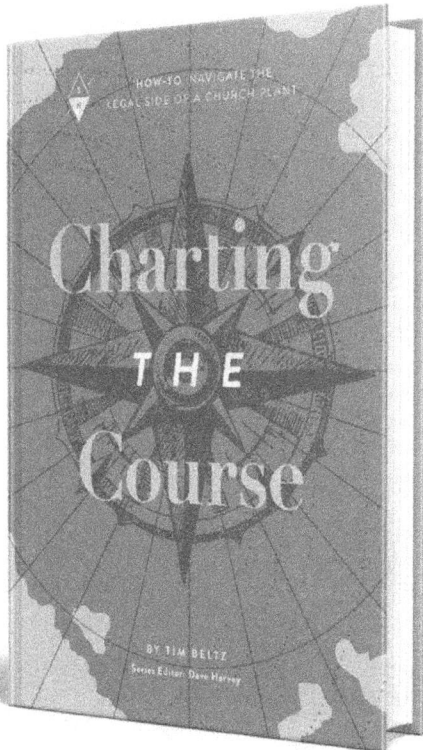

Redemptive Participation: A "How-To" Guide for Pastors in Culture by Mike Cosper

Our culture is confused. And so are we. It's not just you or them. It's all of us. But we can move past confusion and into a place of careful discernment. *Redemptive Participation* brings awareness to the shaping forces in our current culture and how to connect these dynamics with our teaching and practice.

Filling Blank Spaces: "How-To" Work with Visual Artists in Your Church by Michael Winters

In the beginning, the earth was empty. Blank spaces were everywhere. *Filling Blank Spaces* addresses a topic that usually gets blank stares in the church world. But Winters is a seasoned veteran of arts ministry and has developed a premier arts and culture movement in the United States, without elaborate budgets or celebrity cameos. Instead, this guide gives a "How-To" approach to understanding visual art as for and from the local church, steering clear of both low-brow kitsch and obscure couture. If you are ready to start engaging a wider, and often under-reached, swath of your city, while awakening creative force within your local church, then this book is for you.

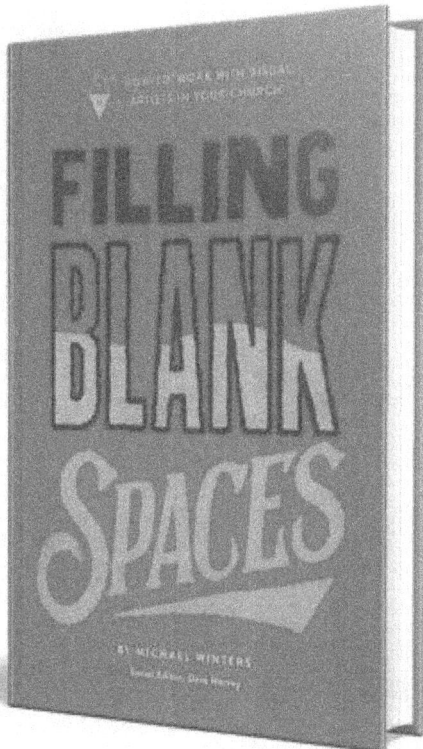

Before the Lord, Before the Church: "How-To" Plan a Child

Dedication Service by Jared Kennedy with Megan Kennedy

Is child dedication just a sentimental moment to celebrate family with "oohs and ahhs" over the babies? Or is it a solemn moment before God and a covenanting one before the local church? Kennedy explains a philosophy of child dedication with poignant "How-To" plan for living out a powerful witness to Christ for one another and before the watching world. Whether you are rescuing various forms of child dedication from sentimentalism or perhaps sacrament, this book will guide you to faithful and fruitful ministry honoring God for the gift of children while blessing your church.

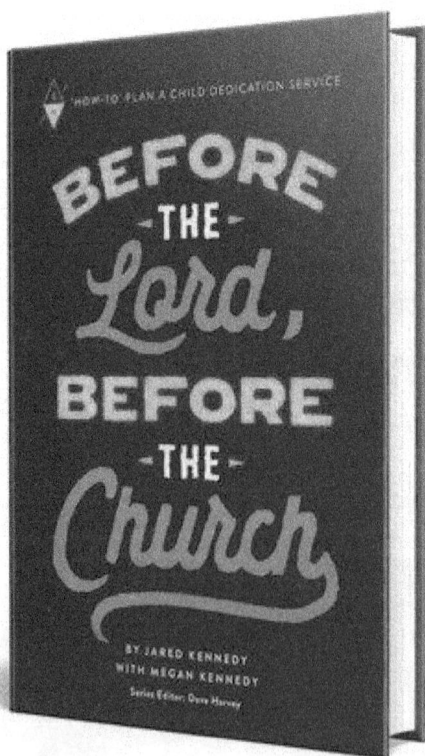

Sabbaticals: "How-To" Take a Break from Ministry before Ministry Breaks You by Rusty McKie

Are you tired and worn out from ministry? Isn't Jesus' burden supposed to be light? In the pressure-producing machine of our chaotic world, Jesus' words of rest don't often touch our life. As ministry leaders, we know a lot about biblical rest, yet we don't often experience it. The ancient practice of sabbath provides ample wisdom on how to enter into rest in Christ. *Sabbaticals* is a guide showing us how to implement Sabbath principles into a sabbatical as well as into the ebb and flow of our entire life.

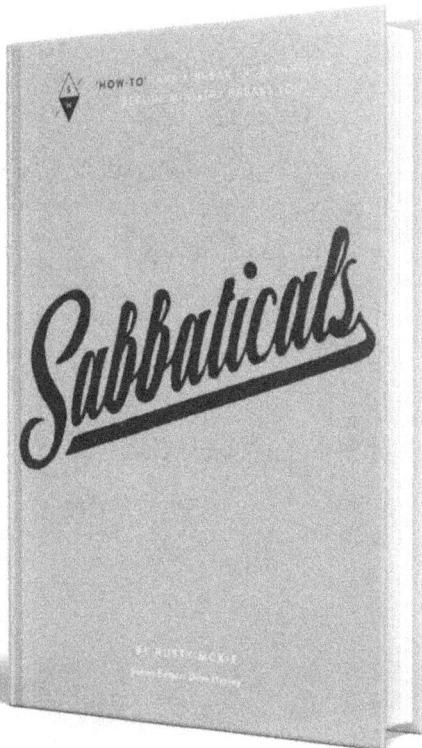

Leaders through Relationship: "How-To" Develop Leaders in the

Local Church by Kevin Galloway

The church needs more godly leaders. But where do they come from? Some people read leadership books in a season of rest and health. But if we're honest, most often we read leadership books when we're frazzled, when we see the problems around us but not the solutions. If you're feeling the leadership strain in your church, let Kevin Galloway show you a way forward, the way of Jesus, the way of personally investing in leaders who then invest in other leaders—because making an intentional plan to encourage and train leaders, is not a luxury; it's mission critical, for your health and the health of your church.

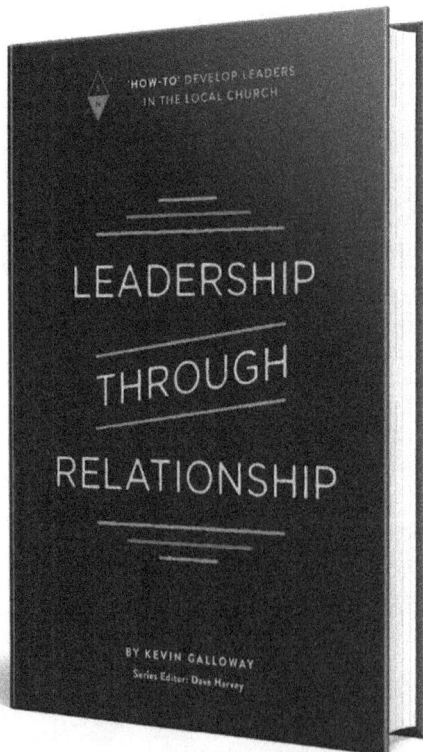

Raising the Dust: "How-To" Equip Deacons to Serve the Church by Gregg Allison & Ryan Welsh (forthcoming)

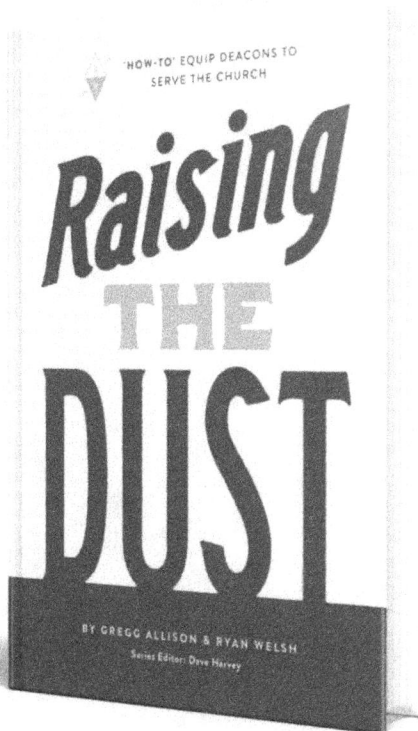

www.ingramcontent.com/pod-product-compliance
Lightning Source LLC
Chambersburg PA
CBHW031627040426
42452CB00007B/712